EDGAR LEE MASTERS

A Centenary Memoir-Anthology

The man from Spoon River
(probably taken about 1915)

Edgar Lee Masters

A Centenary Memoir-Anthology

HARDIN W. MASTERS

South Brunswick and New York: A. S. Barnes and Company
for the
POETRY SOCIETY OF AMERICA

THE CENTENARY SERIES

Volumes in this Series will appear on the occasion of the 100th anniversary of the birth of distinguished past members of The Poetry Society of America. The present Memoir of Edgar Lee Masters is the fifth in the Series. The first Memoir, that of Richard Le Gallienne, was edited by Clarence R. Decker; the second Memoir, that of George Sterling, was edited by Charles Angoff; the third, that of Jessie Rittenhouse, was edited by Margaret Widdemer; the fourth, that of Edwin Arlington Robinson, was edited by Bernard Grebanier.

Library of Congress Cataloging in Publication Data

Masters, Edgar Lee, 1869–1950.
    Edgar Lee Masters; a centenary memoir-anthology.

    (The Centenary series)
    I. Masters, Hardin Wallace, 1899–   ed.
II.   Series: Poetry Society of America.   Centenary series.
PS3525.A83A17   1972   811'.5'2   79-37955
ISBN 0-498-01114-3

A. S. Barnes and Co., Inc.
Cranbury, New Jersey 08512

Printed in the United States of America

To "Kaduker" and his friends

FOREWORD

EDGAR LEE MASTERS was born August 23, 1869,
according to his own statement made to me during one of
my frequent visits to his apartment at the Chelsea Hotel
in New York. If this date is wrong, my father compounded
the error in the opening sentence of his autobiography, pub-
lished in 1936. In any event, the statement is typical of
facets of a life that have become somewhat controversial as
the years flow by. It is a beginning compatible with events
that took place during the early years.

I have not examined the records in Garnett, Kansas, but
there is a plaque on the wall of the old house Father was
born in, which reads:

Edgar Lee Masters 1868–1950. Creative genius, brilliant at-
torney, and beloved native son. A country is not railroads,
grain elevators and factories, but it is the character of the
land, its spirit as shown by its poets and creative minds.

My father's life might be divided into two sections or
portions—either before and after *Spoon River,* or by voca-
tion and avocation. Either designation would be proper to
a better understanding of his inspiration, his writing, and
the impelling forces behind his poetry and his novels.

It is in this context that I humbly present a short intro-
duction to this anthology. Although I have listened to my
share of the family's poetry over the years since *Spoon River*

was written, it would be preposterous of me to pretend to judge it. My approach to verse must be as a *businessman* and as an elder son. It must be purely personal, like preferring lemon in my tea. I like it or I don't like it, but I never know why. The structure, the flow, the imagery, as such, remain hidden threads in the weave of the poem. Nonetheless, over the years, and particularly in the 1930s, it was my good fortune to listen to father's comments, criticisms, and, many times, laughter—*his own,* at his writing. So it is that I can pass along, perhaps, the spirit of his judgment, as I remember it, as a vivid experience and a matter of record in my personal papers. Hopefully, it will also be a matter of interest to the students of verse today, and to those people who admired Masters.

He graduated from Lewistown High School on May 28, 1886, and found life in town to be lonely during his teenage years. However, he subsequently studied law sporadically in his father's law office, and under Hardin Wallace Masters's tutorship.

Many things must, to a degree, influence and control a writer's life. In the case of Edgar Lee Masters, an event to be of great later significance was his marriage to Helen Jenkins on June 21, 1898. She was the daughter of Robert E. Jenkins, well-known member of the Chicago Bar and president of the Metropolitan Elevated Co. in Chicago. At this time Masters had been living in Chicago for about six years, and was a partner of the law firm Scanlan & Masters. It is significant that out of this marriage and law practice came the birth of *Spoon River Anthology,* in a little over ten years after this first marriage.

Much has been written about the person or persons who were the stimuli for this famous book of poetry. Masters's contemporaries about 1914–15 were friends like John Masefield, Edwin Arlington Robinson, Percy MacKaye, and other well-known authors of the time. However, the people responsible for the initial push, the conception, if you will, were his mother, Emma Jerusha Masters, his wife, Helen Jenkins Masters, and outside the family William Marion Reedy and Harriet Monroe, with their great impact on his ambitions. The latter nourished and encouraged my father, who, under the name of Webster Ford had in 1910 privately published a modest little book entitled *Songs and Sonnets.*

So it was that Ford emerged as Masters, and perhaps in prophecy had written the poem "The House in the Woods":

Shadows upon the wall
And a ghost of the past on the floor,
Here where the hours made carnival
In the days that are no more.

Contrary to general belief, my father was not a college graduate. He attended Knox academy on a make-up status for about one year in 1889 but found he was not ready for college even at the age of 21. Nevertheless, he went to Springfield, Illinois, and took the bar examination, standing first in the class of sixty applicants, and was admitted to the practice of law about 1891. It was seven years afterward that he published *A Book of Verses,* under the auspices of Way & Williams of Chicago.

Enough cannot be said on the great affection and push that Bill Reedy gave to the book *Spoon River Anthology.* In *Toward the Gulf* my father wrote, "It would have been fitting had I dedicated SRA to you. Considerations of an intimate nature, not to mention a literary encouragement which was before yours, crowded you from the page."

Thus the point is sufficiently made regarding the people who nurtured and impelled the poet-lawyer or lawyer-poet from unknown sonnets to immortality in verse. But this does not give full credit to father's love of Homer, Greek literature, and specifically to the Greek Anthology, for the "epitaphic form" of *Spoon River.*

I cannot judge poetry on any basis, but I can vividly recall my father's comments on his own poetry. High on the list of his "best" books was *Domesday Book* and, among others, the following poems from other books of his:

"Tomorrow Is My Birthday"   "The Corn"
"Botanical Gardens"   "The Statue"
"The Grand River Marshes" "The Hittites"
"New York"   "In the Garden"
"Worlds"   "Golden Gate Park"

The selections are categorized as Stories in Verse, Lyrics and Sonnets, Dithyrambs, and Poems of Reflection by the author.

Also, a student of Masters must not overlook his novels, like *Mitch Miller* (1920), *Children of The Market Place* (1922), *The Nuptial Flight* (1923), or his *Presentation of Emerson,* published by Longmans, Green and Co. in 1940. All reveal strong, dynamic prose of different moods.

To get back to portions one and two. First in the time-picture will be the youth of central Illinois, and the man who later practiced law to put bread on the table. Second are the *Spoon River* days, the period from about 1910 to 1925—the years of praise, publicity, and great adulation. Then comes the sequel to years of law practice and the genius of the *Spoon River* days. This period might be termed the Chelsea period, and is confined to the years of my father's residence in New York and the East.

Two early books, *Maximillian,* published in 1902, and more particularly the *New Star Chamber,* published in 1904, give a better picture of my father's political philosophy than I possibly can. A good summary is contained in the Foreword of the latter book, and I quote, "Oh Ye People Who Are Free, remember the maxim that liberty may be acquired but never recovered." The *New Star Chamber & Other Essays* (1904), called by my father "a contribution to the literature of liberty," lists among its contents essays on Theodore Roosevelt, John Marshall, Thomas Jefferson, Alexander Hamilton, and Mr. Bryan's Campaigns. So much for two early books.

It has always seemed to me that my father's legal talents— his power and ability to cross-examine witnesses, to delve into the innermost recesses of an individual's motives—made many of his poems possible. In addition to the strictures of the Muse, he was faced with the prosaic and periodic necessity of paying grocery bills, which gave him a sound and earthy base for exploiting the everyday viewpoint. Added to this was a flowing imagination, which, I believe, inspired many of his cultural or artistic decisions. Quite a number of poems are "angry" poems, storming thru death at the injustice of life. They are cynical, hissing recitations.

In 1914 Amy Lowell brought out *Sword Blades and Poppy Seeds,* which was of great interest to Edgar Lee Masters, according to my memoranda. I quote from the preface the portion he marked in her book, because it seems typical and significant of the times in which my father was involved in the new era of American poetry:

For the purely technical side I must state my immense debt to the French, and perhaps above all to the so-called Parnassian School, although some of the writers who have influenced me most do not belong to it. High minded and untiring workmen, they have spared no pains to produce a poetry finer than that of any other country in our time— poetry so full of beauty and feeling, and the study of it at once an inspiration and a despair to the artist. The Anglo-Saxon of our day has a tendency to think that a fine idea excuses slovenly workmanship. These clear-eyed Frenchmen are a reproof to our self-satisfied laziness.

Many times I have heard ELM make a similar comment about the poets of his own country. This was his credo: No excuse for slovenly workmanship.

However, I am attempting to relate the lawyer and the businessman to his philosophy and to his work. Any proper evaluation of this matter must consider some of the following facts, some of the debits and credits:

Many places in the Chicago Loop hold ELM's business and legal footprints: the Ashland Block in 1900, later the Marquette, Monadnock, and Portland buildings.

11

My father was an astute and tough man on cross-examination of witnesses, unexcelled in the writing of briefs, and imaginative in law research.

He was not a pessimist; he believed in the fellowship of man and the individual's aspirations.

He tried ardently to represent his forebears and again believed in responsible individual freedom; by responsible, I mean the obligation of leading a constructive life.

My father opposed centralized government, imperialism, and prohibition.

He had a cosmic faith, was a Jeffersonian democrat, and had no interest in either socialism or communism as a way of life. He was an advocate of state sovereignty. He felt that business and banking controlled the courts and had too much power in the running of the country.

He approved also of an agrarian-based populism.

All of this had a bearing and influence on father's later life and writings, as background to the main event.

As a self-made attorney, Edgar Lee Masters practiced law from 1892 to 1924, eight of these years, 1903 to 1911, with Clarence Darrow, in the Chicago firm of Darrow, Masters and Wilson.

Perhaps I am true to father's memory in saying that the lines, the pathos, the indescribably personal relation of poems such as "Anne Rutledge," "In a Garden," or "Silence" are good examples of his art. Then, again, the man of the four-walled office, the brilliant lawyer, the provider, comes frothing over in the amusing lines of "Slip Shoe Lovey" from *The Great Valley*, published in 1916.

One other characteristic of the man, one which enthralled me, is best described by the word *Pantheistic*. He was deeply in love with nature during his entire lifetime, from the days of our Michigan farm to the time when he sat with his beloved father, Hardin Wallace Masters, on the porch in the summer twilight of Springfield, Illinois, and first listened to the stir of the wind in the poplar trees. Even in the drab courtyard that he viewed from his studio at the Chelsea

12

Hotel, a starving catalpa tree claimed his daily comment and affection.

It may be amusing, even laughable, but I suggest that father's intense interest in religion, the Koran, the Bhagavad Gita, and the Bible was perhaps reversed as the years flowed by him: The ardent Christian as a young man became an agnostic in his cynical maturity. I believe that this reversal changed his poetry. He became a free-verse iconoclast.

In these poems, I hope you will join me in the search for all these facets of identity of the man who wrote them. What were the combinations of cosmic rays that made many of them such startling pictures of ourselves? Perhaps you will agree that my father's palette blended the mystic, the agnostic, the farmer, the liberal, the lawyer, and the poet. There is ever a touch of his dedication to the Greek tragedies and to the glory that was Greece. There is a large dash of love for his pioneer antecedents, and for America and the tragic changes in her historical pathway, which he felt were inevitable.

What was the physical appearance of poet Masters during the early years? Well, in my papers are likenesses of him at different times. Let me describe them, in the hope that the reader may see him as I do. A photograph done by Matzene in Chicago about 1900 is indeed the man of law, the poet, the man of dreams and imagination—broad brow; heavy eyebrows; deep-set eyes; a broad nose, flaring at the base; full, sensuous lips; and overall an oval handsome face, crowned by long black hair, parted on the left side. The picture fairly shouts "I have ability and ambition." On his vest is a watch chain with a round locket containing a small diamond in the center. It is the epitome of a serious young man.

And there is a photo by the Gibson Galleries, taken several years later, rather a blueprint of the first. This one emphasizes father's fine hair, full lips, and deep-set eyes under the broad brow.

In 1911 I took a series of Kodaks. These show a slender

13

young man standing in front of his Kenwood Avenue home in the best of spirits—a genial, smiling face, in contrast to the severe pictures of later years.

In his early forties my father was slender and handsome, not to say debonair, in appearance. Later he acquired the corpulence of age, and the eyes, which had been quizzical and not unhappy, became penetrating, cynical, and hard. He had a habit of "looking holes through you," as the saying goes. In talking with him, one felt as if he were on the witness stand under cross examination.

Like all men of artistic capacities, Edgar Lee Masters had great yearning for the beauty in life, and above all for living a life of serenity. He knew that the best and most practical way of attaining this was to be independent financially. He strove mightily to achieve this end, both in his lucrative law practice, and later, in royalties from *Spoon River*. He never quite made it, for he had little understanding of the ways of money. It was only in his Spring Lake, Michigan, farm, and the affluence of his middle forties, that he came close to an independent way of life and a place of peace.

A man of good physique, a constant walker and swimmer, father took excellent care of himself. His stamina proved to be a great asset during the thirty-odd years of practicing law in the daytime and writing at night. When the original *Spoon River* became a best seller, he went on with additional poems from his poetry storeroom. Some of these were used in the *New Spoon River*, published in 1924. Thus his energy and good health were most valuable to his writing career.

Finally, when he deserted the shores of Michigan and the walks of Chicago, when he closed his law books and wrote his last brief, the tempo changed and he never regained it. Who knows what changed the tempo? There were no more *Spoon Rivers* and there was not another *Domesday Book*.

The early 1920s were bitter and tragic years for the author of *Spoon River*. Only five years had elapsed since

Spoon River had been published, but financial and marital storm clouds were on the horizon. My mother and sisters were having a desperate time getting along, many of his intimate friends had been brushed aside, and my father was in trouble with his law practice. *Domesday Book* (1920) was apparently the last of his significant writing for a period of some years. In my opinion he never recovered from his troubles and tribulations in this decade. They were reflected in his income, his social perspective, and his writing.

A part of this period was tied into his law partnership with Clarence Darrow and the firm of Darrow, Masters & Wilson. There were relatively calm, well-ordered, and organized days, the pace being set by a large and prominent law office. However, the Darrow association ended in bitterness and enmity. About this time ELM was occupied with poems that later were published in *Toward the Gulf* (1918) and the *New Spoon River*.

I cannot accurately relate the number or the relative importance of all the women who influenced his thinking, his life, and his writing. Many of his poems, of course, were inspired by some of them. He confided in me occasionally about his emotional involvements, but seldom by name or degree. Suffice it to say, from his earliest days with his school teacher Mary Fisher in Lewistown, Illinois, to his favorite nurse at the Pine Rest Sanitorium when he was 81, he was happy in his relationships with women. Some of his favorites may have been confined to a sexual interest and others to a friendship or affection in kind. It must be emphasized that they played a vital and important part in his creative life.

Masters was an omnivorous reader. His taste ranged from the *Iliad* to Zola, from Balzac to Maeterlinck, and his library contained a wide range of subjects and authors. There was always a book in his pocket. It should be stressed that music was also a part of his cultural fare during his reflective times at the Chelsea Hotel.

One familiar trait of the poet was his sense of humor and love of the ludicrous. He had a great affection for the Negro, as a person and as an artist. He knew many Negroes by name and was happy to clown with them. His affection for them comes through very well, indeed, in a poem like "Dear Old Dick."

Father spent much time in playing the buffoon. His friends received a steady stream of letters from made-up characters like Harley Prowler, Lucius Puckett, Dr. Lucius Atherton, and others. These Rabelaisian epistles glorified Lydia Pinkham's compound, Peruna, and other patent medicines of the day. I have seen my father laugh so hard that he was sometimes unable to post the letter when standing directly in front of the mailbox.

Also involved with him in his lifelong problem with both sudden tears and laughter were a few friends, such diverse men as William Jennings Bryan, Teddy Roosevelt, Charles Gates Dawes, Jack London, Dreiser, H. L. Mencken, and Sandburg (but above all his own father—HWM), to say nothing of his favorite waitress at Henrici's in Chicago.

A few months ago I stood on the farm of my great-grand-father, Squire Davis Masters, near Petersburg, Illinois. The autumn glory of Illinois was on the land and the Mason County hills beckoned on the horizon. I thought of *my* father, *his* father, and *his father's father*, successively: poet-lawyer; lawyer sportsman; and farmer, man of God. I realized the vital influence that Edgar Lee Masters's grand-father had played in his life—farmer, man of God, happy and sufficient unto himself for fifty-seven years on this lovely piece of land (1847–1904).

Long ago I prayed that I might perceive what comes to me today about my father. Much of this now comes back to me in each line of his face and many lines of his pen. I wish I had understood him better when he was here trying to understand me.

It is important to me in this short memoir to recall the

traits of ELM's inmost being that stood out above the rest. One of these was his love of America as he thought it had been or wanted it to be. This affection appears again and again throughout his book and was evident in his many talks with me. Perhaps it is best typified in the following extract from *Invisible Landscapes:*

Give us back our country, the old land,
The cities, villages, and measureless fields
Of toil and song, the just reward and sleep
That follow after labor performed in hope.
But living men, the sons of those who shouldered
A destiny and vision, and strove to be
Light-givers and world makers, not by war,
But by the wise economies of peace.

This was father's 1942 Christmas card to close friends. It is a combination of nostalgic rapture for the old days and his concept of those days.

I would like to strike this chord again by quoting from "Lucinda Matlock" in the *Spoon River Anthology:*

At ninety-six I had lived enough. . . .
What is this I hear of sorrow and weariness,
Anger, discontent and drooping hopes?
Degenerate sons and daughters,
Life is too strong for you—
It takes life to love Life.

If you understand this heroic poetic license, here and in many of my father's poems, you will understand much of his philosophy and talent as a writer.

Masters's genius as reflected in *Spoon River* and *Domesday Book* probably has a greater impact on poetry today than over a half century ago, back in 1915. The vignettes of lives, cynically and realistically portrayed, are eternally woven in the web of tomorrow. Some of the poems could have been written yesterday.

His motto for those he sired was: keep neat and clean, keep physically strong, and don't waste time. Some of our

17

young people today would have found ELM severe, and contemptuous of their way of life and their lack of ambition. Some might even say that he would have attained a greater immortality had he been able to graduate from college . . . but is not immortality a relative matter?

Hardin W. Masters

ACKNOWLEDGMENTS

For inspiration and guidance, my friend, the late

Gustav Davidson

For good friendship and counsel in many and diverse ways

Mrs. M. H. Hutchison
W. A. Logan
Jean Masters
Dr. Thomas D. Masters
Marcia Lee Masters
Mrs. William F. Watts

H.W.M.

19

CONTENTS

ILLUSTRATIONS

EDGAR LEE MASTERS

A Centenary Memoir-Anthology

FROM *SPOON RIVER**

Hannah Armstrong

I WROTE him a letter asking him for old times' sake
To discharge my sick boy from the army;
But maybe he couldn't read it.
Then I went to town and had James Garber,
Who wrote beautifully, write him a letter;
But maybe that was lost in the mails.
So I traveled all the way to Washington.
I was more than an hour finding the White House.
And when I found it they turned me away,
Hiding their smiles. Then I thought:
"Oh, well, he ain't the same as when I boarded him
And he and my husband worked together
And all of us called him Abe, there in Menard."
As a last attempt I turned to a guard and said:
"Please say it's old Aunt Hannah Armstrong
From Illinois, come to see him about her sick boy
In the army."
Well, just in a moment they let me in!
And when he saw me he broke in a laugh,

And dropped his business as president,
And wrote in his own hand Doug's discharge,
Talking the while of the early days,
And telling stories.

Silas Dement

IT was moon-light, and the earth sparkled
With new-fallen frost.
It was midnight and not a soul was abroad.
Out of the chimney of the court-house
A grey-hound of smoke leapt and chased
The northwest wind.
I carried a ladder to the landing of the stairs
And leaned it against the frame of the trap-door
In the ceiling of the portico,
And I crawled under the roof and amid the rafters
And flung among the seasoned timbers
A lighted handful of oil-soaked waste.
Then I came down and slunk away.
In a little while the fire-bell rang—
Clang! Clang! Clang!
And the Spoon River ladder company
Came with a dozen buckets and began to pour water
On the glorious bon-fire, growing hotter,
Higher and brighter, till the walls fell in,
And the limestone columns where Lincoln stood
Crashed like trees when the woodman fells them . . .
When I came back from Joliet
There was a new court house with a dome.
For I was punished like all who destroy
The past for the sake of the future.

Aaron Hatfield

BETTER than granite, Spoon River,
Is the memory-picture you keep of me
Standing before the pioneer men and women
There at Concord Church on Communion day.
Speaking in broken voice of the peasant youth
Of Galilee who went to the city
And was killed by bankers and lawyers;
My voice mingling with the June wind
That blew over wheat fields from Atterbury;
While the white stones in the burying ground
Around the Church shimmered in the summer sun.
And there, though my own memories
Were too great to bear, were you, O pioneers,
With bowed heads breathing forth your sorrow
For the sons killed in battle and the daughters
And little children who vanished in life's morning,
Or at the intolerable hour of noon.
But in those moments of tragic silence,
When the wine and bread were passed,
Came the reconciliation for us—
Us the ploughmen and the hewers of wood,
Us the peasants, brothers of the peasant of Galilee—
To us came the Comforter
And the consolation of tongues of flame!

Chase Henry

IN life I was the town drunkard;
When I died the priest denied me burial

In holy ground.
The which redounded to my good fortune.
For the Protestants bought this lot,
And buried my body here,
Close to the grave of the banker Nicholas,
And of his wife Priscilla.
Take note, ye prudent and pious souls,
Of the cross-currents in life
Which bring honor to the dead, who lived in shame.

William H. Herndon

THERE by the window in the old house
Perched on the bluff, overlooking miles of valley,
My days of labor closed, sitting out life's decline,
Day by day did I look in my memory,
As one who gazes in an enchantress' crystal globe,
And I saw the figures of the past,
As if in a pageant glassed by a shining dream,
Move through the incredible sphere of time.
And I saw a man arise from the soil like a fabled giant
And throw himself over a deathless destiny,
Master of great armies, head of the republic,
Bringing together into a dithyramb of recreative song
The epic hopes of a people;
At the same time Vulcan of sovereign fires,
Where imperishable shields and swords were beaten out
From spirits tempered in heaven.
Look in the crystal! See how he hastens on
To the place where his path comes up to the path
Of a child of Plutarch and Shakespeare.

28

O Lincoln, actor indeed, playing well your part,
And Booth,who strode in a mimic play within the play,
Often and often I saw you,
As the cawing crows winged their way to the wood
Over my house-top at solemn sunsets,
There by my window,
Alone.

Archibald Higbie

I LOATHED you, Spoon River. I tried to rise above you,
I was ashamed of you. I despised you
As the place of my nativity.
And there in Rome, among the artists,
Speaking Italian, speaking French,
I seemed to myself at times to be free
Of every trace of my origin.
I seemed to be reaching the heights of art
And to breathe the air that the masters breathed,
And to see the world with their eyes.
But still they'd pass my work and say:
"What are you driving at, my friend?
Sometimes the face looks like Apollo's,
At others it has a trace of Lincoln's."
There was no culture, you know, in Spoon River,
And I burned with shame and held my peace.
And what could I do, all covered over
And weighted down with western soil,
Except aspire, and pray for another
Birth in the world, with all of Spoon River
Rooted out of my soul?

29

The Hill

WHERE are Elmer, Herman, Bert, Tom and Charley,
The weak of will, the strong of arm, the clown, the boozer,
    the fighter?
All, all, are sleeping on the hill.

One passed in a fever,
One was burned in a mine,
One was killed in a brawl,
One died in a jail,
One fell from a bridge toiling for children and wife—
All, all are sleeping, sleeping, sleeping on the hill.

Where are Ella, Kate, Mag, Lizzie and Edith,
The tender heart, the simple soul, the loud, the proud, the
    happy one?—
All, all, are sleeping on the hill.

One died in shameful child-birth,
One of a thwarted love,
One at the hands of a brute in a brothel,
One of a broken pride, in the search for heart's desire,
One after life in far-away London and Paris
Was brought to her little space by Ella and Kate and Mag—
All, all are sleeping, sleeping, sleeping on the hill.

Where are Uncle Isaac and Aunt Emily,
And old Towny Kincaid and Sevigne Houghton,
And Major Walker who had talked
With venerable men of the revolution?—
All, all, are sleeping on the hill.

They brought them dead sons from the war,
And daughters whom life had crushed,

And their children fatherless, crying—
All, all are sleeping, sleeping, sleeping on the hill.

Where is Old Fiddler Jones
Who played with life all his ninety years,
Braving the sleet with bared breast,
Drinking, rioting, thinking neither of wife nor kin,
Nor gold, nor love, nor heaven?
Lo! he babbles of the fish-frys of long ago,
Of the horse-races of long ago at Clary's Grove,
Of what Abe Lincoln said
One time at Springfield.

Jefferson Howard

My valiant fight! For I call it valiant,
With my father's beliefs from old Virginia:
Hating slavery, but no less war.
I, full of spirit, audacity, courage
Thrown into life here in Spoon River,
With its dominant forces drawn from New England,
Republicans, Calvinists, merchants, bankers,
Hating me, yet fearing my arm.
With wife and children heavy to carry—
Yet fruits of my very zest of life.
Stealing odd pleasures that cost me prestige,
And reaping evils I had not sown;
Foe of the church with its charnel dankness,
Friend of the human touch of the tavern;
Tangled with fates all alien to me,
Deserted by hands I called my own.

Then just as I felt my giant strength
Short of breath, behold my children
Had wound their lives in stranger gardens—
And I stood alone, as I started alone!
My valiant life! I died on my feet,
Facing the silence—facing the prospect
That no one would know of the fight I made.

Fiddler Jones

THE earth keeps some vibration going
There in your heart, and that is you.
And if the people find you can fiddle,
Why, fiddle you must, for all your life.
What do you see, a harvest of clover?
Or a meadow to walk through to the river?
The wind's in the corn; you rub your hands
For beeves hereafter ready for market;
Or else you hear the rustle of skirts
Like the girls when dancing at Little Grove.
To Cooney Potter a pillar of dust
Or whirling leaves meant ruinous drouth;
They looked to me like Red-Head Sammy
Stepping it off, to "Toor-a-Loor."
How could I till my forty acres
Not to speak of getting more,
With a medley of horns, bassoons and piccolos
Stirred in my brain by crows and robins
And the creak of a wind-mill—only these?
And I never started to plow in my life
That some one did not stop in the road

Father about 33 years of age
(probably taken about 1902)
Courtesy Matzene Studio

My father in his favorite role as farm hand
(taken in August 1933 at Hillsdale, N.Y.)

December 11 – 41

Dear Hardin: I was lonely after you went away, but sleep is a cure, and I slept that afternoon a bit, and that night too.

Now Japan will be licked, I am sure. Somehow the Germans will get to Martinique, and from there run in first harm w PO. Yes, we are in for it; and even if we live there are years ahead of struggle and perhaps poverty. I grew up in the terrible aftermath of the Civil War, then came the Spanish war, then the world war, now this, worse than any, what to do but endure? I know nothing but that or suicide. And what's that? Read what Achilles said.

But — the sun shines bright to-day, the sky is blue and clear. My man is idle.

Take keer of yourself. Love to all.

Ever your Pa
E. L. M.

Yes, I'd come to Illinois if I could think of a place and a way, and I may. I hope soon in the mend.

Letter to Hardin W. Masters, dated December 11, 1941

THE LOTUS IN ILLINOIS

Many summers and winters had come and gone,
Then suddenly the empire was wrecked,
When the imperial army met the barbarian foe.
In Yu Chow An Lu-Shan was stationed
With his star-gleaming legions, there where King Chao
Built his gold pagoda, in the days of Tao and peace
And visions.
An Lu-Shan was defeated.
Then passed the jeweled bamboo flute
And pipes of gold. What remained?
The lotus bloomed and spread its leaves like blue smoke;
Still there were crows by the city wall,
Still there were white clouds over the mountains of Chu,
Though the Ku-Su palace was in ruins,
And the capital of Yueh in ruins.

All along the rivers and lakes of Illinois
The lotus is now blooming, making earth appear
As yellow as the moon.
From Peoria to Havana, from Havana to Grafton
Illinois has become a lotus land.
Centuries before it was a lotus land,
When the Indians called the lotus Chinquapin;
And centuries to come the lotus will bloom
Up and down the water-courses of Illinois,
Whatever happens to armies, to cities,
To empires, and the ambitions of conquerors--
As now the lotus does not note
The absence of Marquette, La Salle,
Tecumseh and Black Hawk.

The lotus will never cease to bloom,
The clouds will never cease to sail,
The crows will always fly
Over Starved Rock and the Hills of Bernadotte.

July 29 1941.

— Edgar Lee Masters
Hotel Chelsea, N.Y.C.

Hitherto unpublished poem of Edgar Lee Masters

And take me away to a dance or picnic.
I ended up with forty acres;
I ended up with a broken fiddle—
And a broken laugh, and a thousand memories,
And not a single regret.

Washington McNeely

RICH, honored by my fellow citizens,
The father of many children, born of a noble mother,
All raised there
In the great mansion-house, at the edge of town.
Note the cedar tree on the lawn!
I sent all the boys to Ann Arbor, all the girls to Rockford,
The while my life went on, getting more riches and honors—
Resting under my cedar tree at evening.
The years went on.
I sent the girls to Europe;
I dowered them when married.
I gave the boys money to start in business.
They were strong children, promising as apples
Before the bitten places show.
But John fled the country in disgrace.
Jenny died in child-birth—
I sat under my cedar tree.
Harry killed himself after a debauch,
Susan was divorced—
I sat under my cedar tree.
Paul was invalided from over study,
May became a recluse at home for love of a man—
I sat under my cedar tree.

All were gone, or broken-winged or devoured by life—
I sat under my cedar tree.
My mate, the mother of them, was taken—
I sat under my cedar tree.
Till ninety years were tolled.
O maternal Earth, which rocks the fallen leaf to sleep!

Lucinda Matlock

I WENT to the dances at Chandlerville,
And played snap-out at Winchester.
One time we changed partners,
Driving home in the moonlight of middle June,
And then I found Davis.
We were married and lived together for seventy years,
Enjoying, working, raising the twelve children,
Eight of whom we lost
Ere I had reached the age of sixty.
I spun, I wove, I kept the house, I nursed the sick,
I made the garden, and for holiday
Rambled over the fields where sang the larks,
And by Spoon River gathering many a shell,
And many a flower and medicinal weed—
Shouting to the wooded hills, singing to the green valleys.
At ninety-six I had lived enough, that is all,
And passed to a sweet repose.
What is this I hear of sorrow and weariness,
Anger, discontent and drooping hopes?
Degenerate sons and daughters,
Life is too strong for you—
It takes life to love Life.

Benjamin Pantier

TOGETHER in this grave lie Benjamin Pantier, attorney at
   law,
And Nig, his dog, constant companion, solace and friend.
Down the gray road, friends, children, men and women,
Passing one by one out of life, left me till I was alone
With Nig for partner, bed-fellow, comrade in drink.
In the morning of life I knew aspiration and saw glory.
Then she, who survives me, snared my soul
With a snare which bled me to death,
Till I, once strong of will, law broken, indifferent,
Living with Nig in a room back of a dingy office.
Under my jaw-bone is snuggled the bony nose of Nig—
Our story is lost in silence. Go by, mad world!

Reuben Pantier

WELL, Emily Sparks, your prayers were not wasted,
Your love was not all in vain.
I owe whatever I was in life
To your hope that would not give me up,
To your love that saw me still as good.
Dear Emily Sparks, let me tell you the story.
I pass the effect of my father and mother;
The milliner's daughter made me trouble
And out I went in the world,
Where I passed through every peril known
Of wine and women and joy of life.
One night, in a room in the Rue de Rivoli,
I was drinking wine with a black-eyed cocotte,

And the tears swam into my eyes.
She thought they were amorous tears and smiled
For thought of her conquest over me.
But my soul was three thousand miles away,
In the days when you taught me in Spoon River.
And just because you no more could love me,
Nor pray for me, nor write me letters,
The eternal silence of you spoke instead.
And the black-eyed cocotte took the tears for hers,
As well as the deceiving kisses I gave her.
Somehow, from that hour, I had a new vision—
Dear Emily Sparks!

Petit, the Poet

SEEDS in a dry pod, tick, tick, tick,
Tick, tick, tick, like mites in a quarrel—
Faint iambics that the full breeze wakens—
But the pine tree makes a symphony thereof.
Triolets, villanelles, rondels, rondeaus,
Ballades by the score with the same old thought:
The snows and the roses of yesterday are vanished;
And what is love but a rose that fades?
Life all around me here in the village:
Tragedy, comedy, valor and truth,
Courage, constancy, heroism, failure—
All in the loom, and oh what patterns!
Woodlands, meadows, streams and rivers—
Blind to all of it my life long.
Triolets, villanelles, rondels, rondeaus,
Seeds in a dry pod, tick, tick, tick,

Tick, tick, tick, what little iambics,
While Homer and Whitman roared in the pines?

Henry Phipps

I WAS the Sunday school superintendent,
The dummy president of the wagon works
And the canning factory,
Acting for Thomas Rhodes and the banking clique;
My son the cashier of the bank,
Wedded to Rhodes' daughter,
My week days spent in making money,
My Sundays at church and in prayer.
In everything a cog in the wheel of things-as-they-are:
Of money, master and man, made white
With the paint of the Christian creed.
And then:
The bank collapsed. I stood and looked at the wrecked
    machine—
The wheels with blow-holes stopped with putty and painted;
The rotten bolts, the broken rods;
And only the hopper for souls fit to be used again
In a new devourer of life, when newspapers, judges and
    money-magicians
Build over again.
I was stripped to the bone, but I lay in the Rock of Ages,
Seeing now through the game, no longer a dupe,
And knowing "the upright shall dwell in the land
But the years of the wicked shall be shortened."
Then suddenly, Dr. Meyers discovered
A cancer in my liver.

I was not, after all, the particular care of God!
Why, even thus standing on a peak
Above the mists through which I had climbed,
And ready for larger life in the world,
Eternal forces
Moved me on with a push.

Thomas Rhodes

VERY well, you liberals,
And navigators into realms intellectual,
You sailors through heights imaginative,
Blown about by erratic currents, tumbling into air pockets,
You Margaret Fuller Slacks, Petits,
And Tennessee Claflin Shopes—
You found with all your boasted wisdom
How hard at the last it is
To keep the soul from splitting into cellular atoms.
While we, seekers of earth's treasures,
Getters and hoarders of gold,
Are self-contained, compact, harmonized,
Even to the end.

Anne Rutledge

OUT of me unworthy and unknown
The vibrations of deathless music;
"With malice toward none, with charity for all."

Out of me the forgiveness of millions toward millions,
And the beneficent face of a nation
Shining with justice and truth.
I am Anne Rutledge who sleep beneath these weeds,
Beloved in life of Abraham Lincoln,
Wedded to him, not through union,
But through separation,
Bloom forever, O Republic,
From the dust of my bosom!

Judge Somers

How does it happen, tell me,
That I who was most erudite of lawyers,
Who knew Blackstone and Coke
Almost by heart, who made the greatest speech
The court-house ever heard, and wrote
A brief that won the praise of Justice Breese—
How does it happen, tell me,
That I lie here unmarked, forgotten,
While Chase Henry, the town drunkard,
Has a marble block, topped by an urn,
Wherein Nature, in a mood ironical,
Has sown a flowering weed?

Lois Spears

HERE lies the body of Lois Spears,
Born Lois Fluke, daughter of Willard Fluke,

Wife of Cyrus Spears,
Mother of Myrtle and Virgil Spears,
Children with clear eyes and sound limbs—
(I was born blind).
I was the happiest of women
As wife, mother and housekeeper,
Caring for my loved ones,
And making my home
A place of order and bounteous hospitality:
For I went about the rooms,
And about the garden
With an instinct as sure as sight,
As though there were eyes in my finger tips—
Glory to God in the highest.

Rebecca Wasson

SPRING and Summer, Fall and Winter and Spring
After each other drifting, past my window drifting!
And I lay so many years watching them drift and counting
The years till a terror came in my heart at times,
With the feeling that I had become eternal; at last
My hundredth year was reached! And still I lay
Hearing the tick of the clock, and the low of cattle
And the scream of a jay flying through falling leaves!
Day after day alone in a room of the house
Of a daughter-in-law stricken with age and gray.
And by night, or looking out of the window by day
My thought ran back, it seemed, through infinite time
To North Carolina and all my girlhood days,
And John, my John, away to the war with the British,

And all the children, the deaths, and all the sorrows.
And that stretch of years like a prairie in Illinois
Through which great figures passed like hurrying horsemen,
Washington, Jefferson, Jackson, Webster, Clay.
O beautiful young republic for whom my John and I
Gave all of our strength and love!
And O my John!
Why, when I lay so helpless in bed for years,
Praying for you to come, was your coming delayed?
Seeing that with a cry of rapture, like that I uttered
When you found me in old Virginia after the war,
I cried when I beheld you there by the bed,
As the sun stood low in the west growing smaller and fainter
In the light of your face!

Harmon Whitney

Out of the lights and roar of cities,
Drifting down like a spark in Spoon River,
Burnt out with the fire of drink, and broken,
The paramour of a woman I took in self-contempt,
But to hide a wounded pride as well.
To be judged and loathed by a village of little minds—
I, gifted with tongues and wisdom,
Sunk here to the dust of the justice court,
A picker of rags in the rubbage of spites and wrongs,—
I, whom fortune smiled on! I in a village,
Spouting to gaping yokels pages of verse,
Out of the lore of golden years,
Or raising a laugh with a flash of filthy wit
When they bought the drinks to kindle my dying mind.

41

To be judged by you,
The soul of me hidden from you,
With its wound gangrened
By love for a wife who made the wound,
With her cold white bosom, treasonous, pure and hard,
Relentless to the last, when the touch of her hand,
At any time, might have cured me of the typhus,
Caught in the jungle of life where many are lost.
And only to think that my soul could not re-act,
Like Byron's did, in song, in something noble,
But turned on itself like a tortured snake—
Judge me this way, O world!

Lines Written in the Desplaines Forest

THE sun has sunk below the level plain,
And yet above the forest's leafy gloom
The glory of the evening lightens still.
Smooth as a mirror is the river's face
With Heaven's light, and all its radiant clouds
And shadows which against the river's shore
Already are as night. From some retreat
Obscure and lonely, evening's saddest bird
Whistles, and beyond the water comes
The musical reply, and silence reigns—
Save for the noisy chorus of the frogs,
And undistinguished sounds of faint portent
That night has come. There is a rustic bridge
Which spans the stream, from which we look below
At Heaven above; 'till revery reclaims
The mind from hurried thought and merges it
Into the universal mind which broods
O'er such a scene. Strange quietude o'erspreads
The restless flame of being, and the soul
Beholds its source and destiny and feels
Not sorrowful to sink into the breast
Of that large life whereof it is a part.
What are we? But the question is not solved
Here in the presence of intensest thought;
Where nature stills the clamor of the world

And leaves us in communion with ourselves.
Hence to the strivings of the clear-eyed day
What take we that shall mitigate the pangs
That each soul is alone, and that all friends
Gentle and wise and good can never soothe
The ache of that sub-consciousness which is
Something unfathomed and unmedicined.
Yet this it is which keeps us in the path
Of some ambition, cherished or pursued;
The still, small voice that is not quieted
By disregard, but ever speaks to us
Its mandates while we wake or sleep, and asks
A closer harmony with that great scheme
Which is the music of the universe.

So as the cherubim of Heaven defend
The realms of the unknown with flaming swords,
Thence are we driven to the world which is
Ours to be known through Art, who beckons us
To excellence, and in her rarer moods
Casts shadowy glances of serener lands;
Where all the serious gods, removed from stress
And interruption, build as we conceive;
In fellowship that knows not that reserve
Which clouds the hearts of those who wish to live
As they, in that large realm of perfect mind.

The White City

THE autumnal sky is blue like June's,
    The wooded isle is sere below
Reflected in the still lagoons

Beneath the full noon's brilliant glow.
Around the wondrous buildings show
    Their sculptured roofs and domes and towers,
Like Rome, ere crime had laid her low,
    Ere the rude North's barbaric powers
    O'erwhelmed her art, which now again is ours.

See the triumphal columns crowned
    By Neptunes—see Diana there,
The tense bow ready to rebound;
    And Victory's wings are high in air.
See Liberty within her chair,
    And over all the Republic stands,
With countenance serene and fair,
    The staff and eagle in her hands,
    Whom we adore, because she loosed our bands.

And back of all the Peristyle
    Protects the land against the sea,
And here the flashing fountains smile
    And varied flags float full and free,
A solemn splendor which may be
    The presence of the majestic dead,
Reigns in the air until the knee
    Would bend in reverence, and the head
    Be bowed for truths we have inherited.

Aye, truths and beauty and the power
    Which makes this vision all our own,
Though for a brief and passing hour;
    Aye, all which drove beyond the cone
Of light, of thought, the withered crone
    Old superstition. Plato reared
Within the mind his bruised throne—
    But Bacon o'er the seal of knowledge steered
    And sought out nature where all men had feared.

Then steam grasped ponderous wheels and drove
　　The winged car from shore to shore,
And swifter than the thoughts of love
　　The tense electric wires bore
Their freight of thought the long miles o'er,
　　Till naught was hidden from men's eyes
Where all was miracle before,
　　　　The earth lay conquered and the skies
　　　　Unveiled themselves to man's great enterprise.

Then Justice shook to earth her chains
　　Unfettered now to do her will;
And Liberty expunged the stains
　　Of blood in centuries of ill.
The awakened earth shook off the chill
　　Of darkness as her heart grew warm
To deeds of daring right, and still
　　　　The nations fairer grew of form,
　　　　In that great birth, the child of that fierce storm.

And thus where art and science hoard
　　The trophies of the fruitful years,
The mighty spirits which out-soared
　　The shadows of their trials and tears,
Dante's and Homer's and Shakespeare's
　　Seem hovering in the sun-lit air,
Now when the attentive spirit hears
　　　　The first sighs of the year's despair,
　　　　While sorrow dyes the earth in hues most fair.

Hark! The Ave Maria rings
　　From out yon fretted minaret
Enshadowed by the twilight's wings;
　　Behold the golden sun has set,

46

Ten thousand lamps blaze in the jet
    Of water, shadowed nook, and tree;
Above, the stars again are met.
    This is a heavenly fantasy—
    Ah, that this dream should ever cease to be.

And lo! How white, how glorious
    These fanes and temples now appear;
How pure a mood is now o'er us,
    The evening bell is sweet and clear.
And there by Dian's brow, how near,
    A star shines singly and alone;
Right o'er the dome's symmetric sphere!
    The flags against the sky are blown—
    And all we cherished once is quickly gone.

Walt Whitman

THE earth which gives and takes,
    Which fashions and unmakes
    Whate'er we prize
Has drawn unto her breast
The face which knew her best,
    The kindliest face we had and closed his eyes.
While Aeschylos and Job had gone before,
And all strong inspiration long was o'er
    He struck the harp to ancient melodies.

The great Republic's love
For which he pained and strove

With might and sense;
Whereto he raised his song,
Which drives like leaves along
　　Strong thoughts in storms of primal eloquence,
Grieves for him dead, and clips his flowing hair,
Decks with sweet flowers the place about his bier,
　　For him who has departed bravely thence.

The soul of him who could
Find true in false, and good
　　In everything.
From woman, man and boy
Learned all he knew, took joy
　　In masonry and mines and house-building.
Like those Prometheus taught at wisdom's birth,
Has floated from the shadow of our earth,
　　To heights the mighty reach on dauntless wing.

The eagle eye, which saw
The spirit's worth, the law
　　Of fairer fate
The Nation's final form
Through past and future storm,
　　The fabric of a safe and gracious state,
Is closed by envious death, but not in vain
The vision he projected will remain,
　　To be our life hereafter soon or late.

He knew these pageants pass
As in a magic glass
　　And fill the shade
With substance, which before
Was empty, that no more
　　Is reached than dreamed of, for which men have paid
In hopes and deeds, in virtue and in love,
In every noble thing man dreameth of

In casting off despairs which on him weighed.

He was the truest child,
Our Western world beguiled
    And heaven bestowed.
Vast as our plains of wheat,
Sweet as our winds are sweet
    High as our mountains in the feathery cloud.
As strong as rivers flowing from the west,
Fruitful as California's sea-washed breast
    Broad as the land he made his loved abode.

He flung the past aside
The gods of field and tide
    Of hill and plain.
The green tree was his shrine
To him, all things divine
    The common road, small hamlets, drought and rain.
The Sun, which is Apollo, was his god,
Gave in his hand the gold divining rod
    And said, I clasp the world and have no stain.

In seasons of despair,
In times of poisoned air
    He kept the faith
Of cheerfulness, of strength,
Of man's triumph at length,
    The love of life had given him love of death.
He stretched his hands, he could not know to whom,
With sandals of content he proved the gloom,
    Like fall's first sighs he gave away his breath.

There on the beetling heights,
Above our days and nights
    Our shade and shine.
He is enthroned serene,

The great of old between,
   The guardian of the land he made divine.
What though the great Republic grieveth sore,
For thee her bridegroom hastened on before,
   The pilgrim's bride will leave her hopes for thine.

Ballade of Salem Town

WHERE is the inn of Salem Town
   Where Lincoln loafed ere we knew his name?
When the Clarys from Prairie Grove were down,
   And he kindled mirth with his wit like flame.
   Loud are these things on the lips of fame,
But crumbled to dust is the log-wood wall,
   And perished alike are 'squire and dame—
The toiling year is the Lord of all.
Where is the mill of such renown?
   And the sluice where the swirling waters came?
And the hamlet's sage and the rustic clown
   And those who had glory and those who had shame?
   And those who lost in this curious game;
The bully, the acred-lord and his thrall—
   Gone are they all beyond Time's reclaim—
The toiling year is the Lord of all.

But when jest passed 'twixt laggard and lown
   And the cold wind whined at the window frame,
Then careless alike of smile or frown
   He builded for those who should carp or blame,
   Thereafter when Error should seek to maim
The hand of Liberty in her hall,

When he made Malice and Treason tame—
The toiling year is the Lord of all.

ENVOY

Prince! this shaft of marble is brown
    Ere a cycle is past, and at last will fall
But fame has fashioned his fadeless crown
    The toiling year is the Lord of all.

Helen of Troy

On an ancient vase representing in bas-relief the flight of
Helen.

THIS is the vase of love
    Whose feet would ever rove
O'er land and sea;
Whose hopes forever seek
Bright eyes, the vermeiled cheek,
    And ways made free.

Do we not understand
Why thou didst leave thy land,
    Thy spouse, thy hearth?
Helen of Troy, Greek art
Hath made our heart thy heart,
    Thy mirth our mirth.

For Paris did appear
Curled hair and rosy ear
    And tapering hands.

He spoke—the blood ran fast,
He touched, and killed the past,
   And clove its bands.

And this, I deem, is why
The restless ages sigh,
   Helen, for thee.
Whate'er we do or dream,
Whate'er we say or seem,
   We would be free.

We would forsake old love,
And all the pain thereof,
   And all the care;
We would find out new seas,
And lands more strange than these
   And flowers more fair.

We would behold fresh skies
Where summer never dies,
   And amaranths spring.
Lands where the halcyon hours
Nest over scented bowers
   On folded wing.

We would be crowned with bays,
And spend the long bright days
   On sea or shore;
Or sit by haunted woods,
And watch the deep sea's moods,
   And hear its roar.

Beneath that ancient sky
Who is not fain to fly
   As men have fled?
Ah! we would know relief

From marts of wine and beef,
        And oil and bread.

Helen of Troy, Greek art
Hath made our heart thy heart,
        Thy love our love.
For poesy, like thee,
Must fly and wander free
        As the wild dove.

The Last Good-Bye

WE paused to say good-bye,
As we thought for a little while,
Alone in the car, in the corner
Around the turn of the aisle.

A quiver came in your voice,
Your eyes were sorrowful too;
'Twas over—I strode to the doorway,
Then turned to waive an adieu.

But you had not come from the corner,
And though I had gone so far
I retraced, and faced you coming
Into the aisle of the car.

You stopped as one who was caught
In an evil mood by surprise;
I want to forget, I am trying
To forget the look in your eyes.

Your face was blank and cold,
Like Lot's wife turned to salt.
I suddenly trapped and discovered
Your soul in a hidden fault.

Your eyes were tearless and wide,
And your wide eyes looked on me
Like a Maenad musing murder,
Or the mask of Melpomene.

And there in a flash of lightning,
I learned what I never could prove:
That your heart contained no sorrow,
And your heart contained no love.

And my heart is light and heavy,
And this is the reason why:
I am glad we parted forever,
And sad for the last good-bye.

The House in the Wood

SHADOWS upon the wall
And the ghost of a past on the floor,
Here where the hours made carnival
In the days that are no more.

And the chamber is cold and bare,
And the wax from the taper drips;
But I bury my face in your hair,
And swoon at the touch of your lips.

We went from the house to the wood,
But never a word we spoke;
And an eyrie wind like our mood
Rustled the leaves of the oak.

Dead leaves, tremulous, crisp,
That breathed a forgotten tune;
A cloud the shape of a wisp
Blotted the soaring moon.

Silent we walked the path,
And then the wild farewell;
I saw your form like a wraith
Fade in the forest's dell.

If joy would never depart,
If we could but still the pain—
Dear, I awoke with a pang in my heart
And heard the sound of the rain.

Be with Me through the Spring

THE snow has passed, the crocus blooms,
A swelling tide of life returns;
Green lights invade the forest glooms,
All nature wakes and yearns.
The breeze lifts and the ships take wing
To havens which we long have known;
And yet—and yet I dread the spring,
For fear you may be gone.

Life gives us sweet delights and then

Gathers them back and buries them deep.
Oh, wanton hearts, that kill them when
They do not tire or sleep.
The breeze lifts and the ships take wing—
Be with me through the spring.

Ballad of Life and Love

SHE came to me when Time was gray,
And the mists were on the sea.
She said, "Come, take me by the hand
And walk the world with me."

Her soul was like the morning dew,
Her eyes were deep with dreams,
Her heart beat like the falling wind
In a place of leaves and streams.

I took her hand, uprose the mist,
And merrily shone the sun;
We wandered till the morning came
And till the day was done.

Her voice was murmurous like the sea,
Her voice was sweet with truth;
She kissed me on the eyes and lips
And said, "Take back thy youth."

We crossed a magic meadowland
And rested by a grove,
And then she handed me a lute—
Alas! the lute of Love!

"Oh, sing to me the bitter pain
When I am gone, and when
The summer of a desolate day
Walks down the earth again.

"Oh, sing to me the depth of life,
The sorrow of dead dreams."
And then her heart beat like the wind
In a place of leaves and streams.

"Oh, sing the warning bell that rings
Beside a treacherous reef,
When two souls cling lest morning come,
Yet fall asleep from grief."

Her eyes were like two stars of even;
She said—take heed hereof:
"The lute shall leave thy hands before
Thy heart gives up its love."

I looked to see what demon power
Her soul had come upon;
An evening zephyr shook the trees—
I looked, but she was gone.

The sickle moon hung in the sky,
And the grove was dark and mute;
I stretched my hand to touch the strings—
But vanished was the lute.

The night came down with many stars,
And then I wished for day.
"Oh, fair, oh, sweet, to take the lute,
The lute I learned to play!"

I sang of all she bade me sing,

But oh, the waking pang!
There was no song we did not live,
And all was life I sang.

She came to me when Time was gray,
And the mists were on the sea.
I did not know these things before
She walked the world with me.

I had not heard the bell that warns
The ships against the reef.
Nor clung to one lest morning come,
Yet fall asleep from grief.

I had not heard the undertone
That runs the world around,
That life is bitter, love is deep
And hard to keep if found.

Her voice was murmurous like the sea,
Her voice was sweet with truth;
She kissed me on the brow and cried,
"Evanished is thy youth!"

"For you my heart beats like the wind
In a place of leaves and streams;
I pass to take my place among
The shadows of dead dreams."

Eros Unconquerable

ALL a man hath he will give for his life or love;
Honor and riches shall fail
When her eyes meet his, her hands take his and move
His cheeks to redden and pale.

Wisdom is sweet, and the treasured lore of the wise,
And the words that the seër saith;
But they melt as a cloud at the dazzling look of her eyes,
And her lips' melodious breath.

Her eyelids tremble, the veins in her temple beat,
Her words are soft as a flute.
She stretcheth her hands, the hands of me to entreat,
And time and the world are mute—

Faded and fallen afar in a nebulous inane
At the touch of her finger tips;
There is naught but our hearts that throb with ecstatic pain,
And the blinding kiss of her lips.

All a man hath he will give if herself she give,
Hurt him in flesh and bone,
Custom hath no power o'er him whether he die or live
If her heart be his heart alone.

In this cup I dissolve all the world! Man shall pass
Ere the hour of his joy passeth by:
Let us turn from the darkness and dust—fill the glass,
We will drink to our love ere we die.

Eternal Woman

WITHIN her face I read myself
Remembered, passed from thought;
She is the hope that spurred my youth,
She is the grace I sought.
Her tears reveal the good I missed,
And blot the ill I wrought.

Amidst these later years I stood
Where souls laugh down their care.
Here it was strange again to see
Love's vernal face and fair;
She is the Life that brought to life
Youth's wild and sweet despair.

A languid bliss, a vanished dream,
Her eyes make new and sweet.
She soothes with words a thwarted heart
Lettered in time's defeat.
She is the hyaline cup that makes
The quiet pulses beat.

Between us pass the arisen years
And wounded joys restore.
All shy delights, all wingéd moods,
Open for her the door.
She is the Nereid voice that woke
Music's forgotten lore.

She is the mystery of the world
Strayed out from heaven above.
The light that lures beyond the sky
The souls foredoomed to rove.
And if she slay us it is well,
For she is Life and Love.